Sept 29/02

To Nicholas on your christening day. Enjoy these Bible stories. May you always know God's love.

Love Auntie Ellen, Uncle Jeff, James, Clare & Grace

oxox.

Bible
Stories for Children

First published in 1992 by Brimax

This edition first published in Great Britain in 2002 by Brimax, an imprint
of Octopus Publishing Group Ltd, 2-4 Heron Quays, London E14 4JP

© Octopus Publishing Group 2002

Scripture quotations are taken from the Revised Standard Version of
the Bible © 1946, 1952, 1971 by the Division of Christian Education of the
National Council of Churches of Christ in the USA and used by permission.

ISBN 1 85854 477 7

Printed in France

A CIP catalogue record for this book is available from the British Library.

Bible
Stories for Children

Introduction

In this book we have chosen some of the stories from the Bible for children to read and enjoy.

The Bible, an important historical document, was written by many people over hundreds of years. It has become the most famous of all books.

There are hundreds of stories in the Bible, which is divided into two main parts; the Old Testament and the New Testament.

The Old Testament was originally written in Hebrew and tells the story of the Jewish people. The New Testament was originally written in Greek and tells the story of Jesus.

Contents

Millions of years ago, darkness was everywhere. There was no earth and no sky. There were no seas, no plants, no animals and no people.

In the beginning, God created the heavens and the earth. God said, "Let there be light," and there was light. God separated the light from the dark and called the light day and the dark night.

Then God created the
seas and the sky and the
dry land. Next God
commanded that the
earth produce plants,
trees and flowers of
every kind. All this took
three days.

On the fifth day God created every
living creature. There were fish of
every kind to live in the seas, and
birds to sing and fly in the sky.
There were insects,
reptiles and animals.
God blessed them all and
told them to multiply
and fill the seas, the sky
and the earth.

Then God created man
and woman in his own
image and he blessed
them both. God had
worked very hard for six
days and was pleased
with all he had created.
On the seventh day he
rested and he blessed
this special day.

NOAH'S ARK

Once, long ago, there lived an old man called Noah. He was a good man who loved God. One day, Noah started cutting trees into planks of wood. Many people stood and watched him, in order to see what he was making.

Noah had not told anyone why he was cutting the wood. Even his wife and his sons did not know. At last, after several days, they realised he was making a very large and strong boat.

"How will it float when there is no water nearby?"
"Why are you making it?"
"What is it for?"
These were the questions Noah's family asked him. Noah said, "This is my ark. It will have a door in the side and a roof. It will have a window and three decks."

"God has told me to make the ark," said Noah to his wife. "He is going to send rain to cover the land. His people have been wicked and so every living thing will die. We must go inside the ark with our sons and their children. We must take two of every kind of animal with us. When the water comes, the ark will float and we will all be safe."

"We will need food for ourselves and food for the animals," said Noah's wife. So Noah, his wife and their three sons began to make plans for their stay on the ark. Sacks of grain and salt were stored on the ark. Barrels were filled with fresh water for drinking. Hay and straw were laid in the ark for the animals.

They found two of every animal and loaded them into the ark. There were elephants, lions and camels. There were dogs, cats, birds, snakes and even mice and insects.

Noah could see the rain coming so he closed the doors. Soon, huge, black clouds filled the sky and the rain began to fall. Day after day it rained, until the land was covered by water. As the water rose the ark began to float. The rain fell for forty days and forty nights.

At last the rain stopped and there was a strong wind. But the land was covered with water for five months. There was very little room for the animals. Noah and his family waited patiently for the water to go down.

Gradually the water went down. The ark came to rest on a mountain called Ararat. Noah looked out over the water. He wondered whether it was safe to leave the ark or not.

Noah decided to send out a raven. It did not return. "I will wait a little longer," said Noah.

A week later Noah sent out a dove. But the little dove flew back to the ark for some food. He waited another week then he sent the dove out again. As night fell Noah saw the dove returning to the ark. In its beak it held a green olive leaf. Still Noah waited. The next week the dove did not return. "It is now time to leave the ark," said Noah.

The door of the ark was opened and
Noah and his family came out. The
animals and birds were glad to be
free again. God had saved Noah and
his family from the flood. They all
gave thanks to God.
Across the sky was a beautiful
rainbow. This was a sign from God
that He would never flood the whole
world again.

Can you find any of these in the pages of the story?

dog

Noah

elephant

Noah's wife

raven

dove

rainbow

ark

MOSES

Moses was tending sheep one day on the lower slopes of Horeb, the mountain of God, when he saw a bush on fire. As he watched the fire, he noticed that the flames did not burn the bush. Moses was afraid.

Then he heard a voice coming from the bush. Moses knew it was the voice of God. God told Moses that He wanted him to go to Egypt and rescue the Israelites, who were suffering as slaves there. God wanted Moses to lead them out of Egypt to a new land flowing with milk and honey.

Moses was afraid that the people would not follow him and that Pharaoh, King of Egypt, would not let the people go. God promised to help Moses. Moses travelled to Egypt with his family and on the way he met his brother Aaron whom God had sent to help him. When they reached Egypt, they spoke to the Israelite leaders and told them that God was going to rescue the people. Moses would then lead them to the promised land.

Then Moses spoke to the Pharaoh. "The Lord God of Israel says that you must free his people," said Moses. Pharaoh replied, "Who is this God? I do not know him. I will not let his people go."

Moses asked God for help. God said to Moses, "Pharaoh has refused to free my people. Go and strike the river Nile with your staff and all the water will be changed to blood. The fish will die and there will be no water to drink."

Moses did as God commanded. Still Pharaoh would not let the people go. Next God sent a plague of frogs, after that a plague of mosquitos, then a plague of flies. After each plague Pharaoh was asked to free the Israelites but still he refused. So God sent more plagues to persuade him to change his mind.

God sent a sickness which made all the animals die. Next He sent a plague of dust that turned to boils when it touched the skin of the Egyptians. Then came a great hailstorm. Thunder roared and lightning flashed. Hail the size of rocks fell from the sky, killing men in the fields and destroying the plants and trees. Next a plague of locusts covered the land and ate what remained of the plants and the fruit on the trees. Not a green thing remained in the land of Egypt, but still Pharaoh refused to free the people of Israel.

Then God said to Moses, "Stretch out your hand towards heaven that there may be darkness over the land." Moses did as God told him and the land was plunged into darkness. It was dark for three days.

Again Moses went to see Pharaoh. Pharaoh was very angry. "Get out and never let me see you again," he said to Moses. "I will never let your people go."

God sent one last plague down upon Egypt. He told Moses, "The people will be safe if they do as I tell you."

Moses spoke to the people and told them to listen carefully.

"Tonight," he said, "God's angel of death will pass through Egypt killing the eldest child in every family. To be safe you must kill a young lamb and spread its blood on the door of your house. The meat must be roasted and eaten tonight. You must all stay indoors. The blood on the doors of your houses will be a sign to God that you are His people and He will not let the angel of death harm you. You must remember this night forever and celebrate it as the Passover feast — the time when the angel of death passed over your houses but killed the children of Egypt."

That night when the people of Israel heard the Egyptians cry out, they knew that God had done as He had said and had killed the eldest child in every Egyptian house.

Pharaoh sent for Moses and Aaron and told them to go and take the people with them.

At last the people were free and thousands followed Moses out of Egypt.

God showed Moses the way through the desert by day with a pillar of cloud and by night with a pillar of fire. Soon they came to the Red Sea where they made camp.

When Pharaoh heard that all the people had left and there were no slaves to do the work, he ordered his army and six hundred chariots to follow the people and bring them back to slavery in Egypt.

When the people of Israel saw the army in the distance they were terrified. They were trapped between the Egyptian army on one side and the Red Sea on the other. Moses said, "Do not be afraid. God will save us."

God told Moses to hold
his staff over the water.
Moses did as he was
told. A strong east wind
blew up and made the
sea bed dry land with
great walls of water on
either side. The pillar of
cloud moved behind the
people of Israel and in
front of the Egyptians.
The people of Israel were
able to walk across the
dry sea bed. They
walked all night with the
light from the pillar of
fire to guide them.

53

The Egyptians followed.
As soon as all the people
of Israel were safely
across, God told Moses
to hold his staff over the
sea again.

Once again Moses did as
he was told. The great
walls of water collapsed
and the Egyptian army
and all their chariots
were covered by the sea.
Every man and beast
was drowned.

Moses and the people
were safe and gave
thanks to God who had
rescued them from the
Egyptians.

God provided both food and water
for the people on their journey to
Canaan, the promised land.
Water in stagnant pools was made
safe to drink when God instructed
Moses to throw a log into the water
Another time water came out of dry
rock when Moses struck the rocks
with his staff.

God made bread rain
down from heaven and
quails covered the
ground providing meat.
But no one was allowed
to gather either meat or
bread on the seventh
day, which was the day
of rest called the
Sabbath.

Three months later they reached the foot of Mount Sinai and made camp. This was where God had told Moses to go to Egypt, free the people and lead them to the promised land. Moses climbed the mountain to speak to God. God told Moses to tell the people that as long as they obeyed Him and kept his laws He would always look after them.

God said that He would speak to the people on the morning of the third day. Moses told the people what God had said.

On the morning of the third day, the mountain shook and was covered with smoke and fire. Moses spoke and God answered him in thunder and told him to come again to the top of the mountain.

Moses climbed to the top of the mountain and God spoke of the laws which all must obey.

These laws were the Ten Commandments.

YOU MUST NOT WORSHIP OTHER GODS	*The First Commandment* God said, "I am the Lord your God. You shall have no other God but me."
YOU MUST NOT MAKE IMAGES TO WORSHIP	*The Second Commandment* You must not worship statues or pictures. Only God Himself.
YOU MUST NOT TAKE GOD'S NAME IN VAIN	*The Third Commandment* You must not swear using the name of God. You must not use God's name in c disrespectful way.
YOU MUST KEEP THE SABBATH DAY HOLY	*The Fourth Commandment* This means that we can work for six days but the seventh day, the Sabbath day, must be a day of rest. God Himself created the world in six days and on the seventh day He rested God intended the seventh day for worshipping Him.

YOU MUST RESPECT YOUR FATHER AND MOTHER	**The Fifth Commandment** This means that you must listen to your parents and care for them.
YOU MUST NOT KILL	**The Sixth Commandment** It is wrong to murder.
YOU MUST NOT COMMIT ADULTERY	**The Seventh Commandment** When a man and woman marry they promise to stay together and be faithful to one another. This commandment means being loyal to the one you love.
YOU MUST NOT STEAL	**The Eighth Commandment** It is wrong to take something that is not yours.
YOU MUST NOT TELL LIES	**The Ninth Commandment** It is wrong to tell lies.
YOU MUST NOT COVET	**The Tenth Commandment** To covet means to want something that is not yours. It is wrong to be jealous of another person and to want what belongs to them.

God gave Moses more laws to
guide the people. These laws show
the people how they must love God
and teach their children to love
God and one another.
God gave Moses the
Ten Commandments
written on tablets of
stone.

All these appear in the pages of the story.
Can you find them?

burning bush

pillar of fire

Pharaoh

Moses

DAVID AND GOLIATH

David was a shepherd boy. Every day he looked after his father's sheep and made sure none were stolen. If a wild animal came close, David chased it away. David had seven brothers, but he was the youngest and very proud of his important job.

One day, David was tending the sheep and playing his harp. He saw one of his father's servants, who called out to him, "You must go to your father's house at once. There is someone there who wants to meet you. I will look after the sheep while you are gone."

David ran all the way home. David's father was talking to a strange man. "This is Samuel," said David's father. "He has something special to tell you." Samuel knew that one day David would be King. He wanted to be sure that David would be a good King to his people. He talked to David about this, and told him that when he grew up he would be a great ruler. David was surprised, but he listened carefully.

At that time, King Saul was the ruler of the country. He was a wicked man and not a good king. He was often moody and unhappy. His servants tried to find some entertainment for him.

So David was asked to go to the palace and play his harp for King Saul. The beautiful music made the King much happier. "I want you to stay at the palace and play for me every day," he said to David.

David liked being at the palace, but soon war broke out and King Saul gathered his army together. David went home to his father. Three of David's brothers were in the army and one day, he took some food to them.

While David was talking to his
brothers, there was a loud shout and
a huge man walked out from the
enemy lines. He was as big as a
giant. "Who will fight me?" he
roared. "The man who beats me will
have won the war; but if I win, then
this whole army is in our power."

"Who will fight him?" asked David.
"No one dares to fight Goliath," said
one of his brothers.

David ran to see King Saul. "I will fight Goliath," he said. "But you are only a boy!" said the King. "You cannot fight Goliath." "I may be small," said David, "but with God's help I have killed bears and lions when they came to steal my father's sheep. Please let me try." King Saul finally agreed.

David took his sling and went to a
small stream. He chose five small
stones from the bottom and put them
in his bag. Then he walked towards
Goliath. Goliath laughed when he
saw how small David was. He
charged towards the boy. David took
one of the stones and put it in his
sling. He spun the sling around his
head, then let it go. The stone flew
through the air and hit Goliath in the
middle of his forehead. The giant
man crashed to the ground like a
fallen tree.

All King Saul's soldiers cheered. David
had won the war for them. The
enemy began to run away. King Saul
asked David to stay at the palace.
"My son Jonathan will keep you
company," he said. David was glad
to stay at the palace, and he and
Jonathan became the best of friends.

All these appear in the pages of the story.
Can you find them?

David

King Saul

Samuel

Goliath

sheep

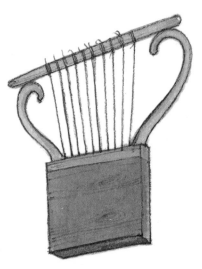

sling

stones

harp

85

Daniel in the Lions' Den

Many years ago, the city of Jerusalem was attacked and conquered by King Nebuchadnezzar of Babylon. He returned home with treasure from the Temple of Jerusalem and a group of young men. He wanted to teach these young men about the ways of Babylon.

Among these young men was a boy called Daniel and his three friends Shadrach, Meshach and Abednego. They worked hard and learned all they were taught. King Nebuchadnezzar offered them food and drink from his own table. The four young men preferred the simple diet of their homeland and this pleased God, as it showed how all four remained loyal to Him. God then gave Daniel the power to understand peoples' dreams.

One night, King Nebuchadnezzar had a dream which worried him. He called together all his wisemen but no one could explain about the dream. The king was angry and sentenced all his wisemen to death.

When Daniel heard what had happened, he prayed to God for help, then went to see the king.

"I will explain your dream," he said. "You saw a giant statue with a golden head. Its body was made of silver and bronze, its legs and feet of iron and clay. As you looked at the statue, a stone fell on it and smashed it into pieces. Then a stone mountain grew in the statue's place. The statue is your kingdom, which will be conquered and destroyed. The stone mountain is the Kingdom of God, which will grow stronger and stronger and will last forever."

King Nebuchadnezzar could not forget
his dream. He decided to make
himself a statue of gold and set it up
outside the city. When his craftsmen
had finished work on the statue, the
king ordered all the people of
Babylon to gather outside the city
and worship the statue.
"When you hear the sound of
trumpets," ordered the king, "you
must kneel and worship the statue."
As the trumpets sounded, everyone
fell to their knees, except for three
men, Shadrach, Meshach and
Abednego.

When the king heard how his order had been disobeyed, he was furious. "If you do not kneel and worship the statue, you will be thrown into a blazing furnace," he cried.
But the three men remained loyal to God and would not kneel.

King Nebuchadnezzar ordered the furnace to be made even hotter than usual. Shadrach, Meshach and Abednego were tied up and thrown into the flames. The heat was so strong that even the guards who threw the men into the furnace were killed by the fire.

The king watched in amazement. "How many men were thrown into the fire?" he asked his servants.

"Three, your majesty," the servants replied.

"I can see four men," said the king. "None are tied up or hurt in any way. The fourth man looks like an angel of God."

The king was right. An angel had been sent by God to protect the three men. When they stepped unhurt from the flames, the king said, "Your God is great."

Some time later, King Nebuchadnezzar had another dream. He saw a great tree which grew bigger and bigger. It could be seen from all over the world and provided everyone with food and shelter. Then an angel came from God and told the king to cut down the tree.

"What does this dream mean?" the king asked Daniel.

Daniel told the king, "Your dream fills me with sadness. You are that tree, providing people with food and protection. But unless you obey God, your power will be taken away and you will become mad."

The king ignored Daniel's words and one day, a terrible madness overcame him. He was thrown out of the city and went to live in the woods and fields. The madness lasted for many years until one day, the king realised that God was more powerful than any king, and was healed.

When King Nebuchadnezzar died, his son Belshazzar became king. He held a great feast and everyone ate and drank from the treasure King Nebuchadnezzar had stolen from the Temple of Jerusalem. As they ate, a hand appeared and wrote a message on the wall. The king was very frightened. He called for Daniel to tell him the meaning of this. Daniel said, "God is not pleased with you. This message means that your kingdom will be conquered by your enemies." That night, King Belshazzar was murdered.

Then Darius became king. He had been an enemy of Belshazzar. He made Daniel ruler over all his governors, because he knew that Daniel was wiser than anyone else in Babylon. The governors were jealous of Daniel and they plotted against him.

A group of governors went to see King Darius. They had a new law for him to sign. This forbade the people to pray to any god for the next thirty days. Anyone found breaking the law would be thrown to the lions. King Darius agreed to sign the law.

Daniel heard about the new law, but he continued to pray to God. One day, his enemies caught him praying. He was taken to the king, who was upset to learn that Daniel had broken the law. He wanted to help Daniel, but knew that he must go to the lions.

King Darius went with Daniel to the lions' pit. He said, "I hope your God can save you."
Then Daniel was thrown into the pit. King Darius returned to the palace and prayed all night for Daniel's safety.

The next morning, the king returned to the pit. "Are you there, Daniel?" he called.
"Yes, I am safe," replied Daniel. "God sent His angel to protect me from the lions' jaws."
The king was very happy that Daniel was safe.

King Darius realized that he had been tricked into signing the law. All the wicked governors who had plotted against Daniel were thrown into the lions' pit. The lions tore them to pieces.

Then King Darius made a new law, saying that all the people in his kingdom must worship the God of Daniel, for He is the the true God.

All these appear in the pages of the story.
Can you find them?

Daniel

Meshach

Shadrach

Abednego

King Nebuchadnezzar

King Belshazzar

King Darius

angel

JONAH AND THE WHALE

There once lived a young man called Jonah. One day, God said to him, "I want you to go to the city of Nineveh. You must tell the people there to change their wicked ways. Unless they do this, I will punish them by destroying their city."

Jonah did not want to go to Nineveh. "If I do go," he said to God, "the people there may change their ways and then you will forgive them. Such cruel and wicked people do not deserve to be forgiven." So Jonah ran away to the sea port of Joppa. There he found a ship sailing to Tarshish, a long way from Nineveh.

Soon after the ship set sail, Jonah fell asleep. But God was not pleased with him. He made the ship sail into a mighty storm. The sailors threw some of their cargo overboard to make the ship easier to control, but the storm became worse.

The sailors began to pray to their
gods for help. The captain of the ship
went below deck and found Jonah
fast asleep.
"Wake up!" he cried. "Pray to your
god as we are praying to ours.
Otherwise we will all drown."

The storm raged on. The sailors decided to draw lots to find out who was to blame for the storm. "Someone has brought us bad luck," they said. Everyone on board wrote down his name then one name was drawn. The chosen name was Jonah!

"What have you done to cause this storm?" asked the sailors.

"I have disobeyed God," said Jonah. "I am trying to run away from Him. The only way to stop this storm is to throw me into the sea."

The sailors did not want to harm Jonah. They tried once more to row the ship back to land, but it was impossible. They had no choice but to throw Jonah into the sea.

The sailors prayed to God. "Please forgive us for throwing this man into the sea." Then they picked Jonah up and tossed him into the waves. At once the winds died down and the sea became calm.

Jonah was afraid he was
going to drown and he
prayed to God. God sent
a huge whale which
swallowed Jonah up.
Jonah was very thankful
that he had not
drowned. He spent three
days and three nights
inside the belly of the
whale. All the time he
prayed to God, thanking
Him for saving his life.

Then God spoke to the whale and the whale put Jonah safely ashore.

Then God spoke to Jonah a second time. "You must go to Nineveh," He said. "Tell the people they must change their wicked ways, or I will punish them." This time Jonah obeyed God.

When Jonah arrived in Nineveh, he began to preach God's message. All the people listened to him, even the King.

The people of Nineveh decided to change their ways. They all prayed to God for forgiveness.
When God saw this, He was pleased and He forgave the people. "I will not harm Nineveh," He said.

Jonah was angry at this. He said to God, "I ran away from you because I was afraid that you would forgive these wicked people. Why forgive those who deserve to be punished?"

Jonah left Nineveh and settled down. He watched the city. He hoped God would change His mind and punish the people after all. God made a plant grow to give Jonah some shade from the fierce sun. Jonah was very grateful for the shade.

The next day, God sent a worm to eat the plant and soon it died. As the sun grew hotter, Jonah became more uncomfortable and more angry. He asked God to let him die. "Are you angry because the plant has died?" asked God.

"Yes, I am," said Jonah. God replied, "You are upset that one plant has died. How do you think I felt about destroying the city of Nineveh? I have cared for the people for many years and now they have changed their ways. They all deserve to be forgiven."

All these appear in the pages of the story.
Can you find them?

ship

Jonah

cargo

sailor

whale

King

plant

city

THE BIRTH OF JESUS

Long ago in a small town called Nazareth, there lived a young girl named Mary. At that time many people had forgotten about God, so He decided to send a little child to live and grow up among the people. This little child would teach them about God.

God knew that Mary loved Him, so He chose her to be the mother of His child. He sent an angel called Gabriel to tell Mary about the baby. She was very frightened when she saw the angel standing near her.

The angel smiled and said, "Do not be afraid, Mary. God has sent me to tell you some good news. Soon you will have a baby. It will be a boy and his name will be Jesus. He will be a holy child, for he will be the Son of God."

A carpenter called Joseph also lived in Nazareth. He loved Mary and wanted to take care of her and the baby. So Joseph took Mary to be his wife.

King Herod decided that he wanted everyone to be counted, so Mary and Joseph had to return to the place where they were born. It was a very long way to go. Mary rode on a donkey and Joseph walked along beside her. At last they arrived and tried to find somewhere to stay.

They were very tired and they both needed to rest. Joseph knocked on the door of an inn. "Have you a bed for the night?" Joseph asked the innkeeper. "My wife is very tired. We have come a long way."

"I am very sorry," said the inn-keeper, shaking his head. "There are no rooms left here. The only thing I can offer you is the stable, if you don't mind sharing with the animals. It is warm and dry."

"Thank you," said Joseph. "That will do very well."

They followed the inn-keeper, who led them out to the stable. Later that night, in the stable with the animals, the baby Jesus was born.

Mary had nothing for the baby to wear, so she wrapped him in strips of cloth. There was nowhere for the baby to sleep, so Joseph placed some soft straw in a manger and made a little bed for the baby Jesus. Mary gently laid the baby down in the manger to sleep.

Outside, on a nearby hillside, some shepherds were looking after their sheep. It was a cold, dark night, so they all sat close to the fire trying to keep warm. Suddenly, a great light shone in the sky and an angel stood before them.

They were all frightened, but the angel said, "Do not be afraid, for I have some good news to tell you. Tonight the Lord Jesus has been born. You must go to him. Follow the bright star and it will lead you to the stable where he lies." Then suddenly the sky was filled with angels singing.

"Glory to God in heaven,
Peace on earth
And Joy to all men."

The shepherds left at once and
followed the star which led them to
the stable. They took their sheep with
them. The shepherds knocked on the
stable door and Joseph let them in. All
the shepherds knelt beside the baby
because they knew he was very
special. Then the shepherds went to
the town to tell everyone about the
birth of the Lord Jesus.

Some wise men had been watching the stars. They knew a great king was to be born. At last they saw the bright star, which they followed across many lands. They thought they would find the new king in a palace, so they went to the palace of King Herod.

King Herod was angry to hear of this new king. He said to the wise men, "When you find this king, you must tell me where he is so I can worship him, too." In fact Herod wanted to kill Jesus.

The wise men finally found Jesus in a stable, asleep in the manger. They knew at once that he was the king they had been waiting for. Each wise man had a gift for Jesus which they laid down beside him — gold, frankincense and myrrh.

That night the wise men had a strange dream. In the dream, God told them not to return to King Herod as he meant to harm Jesus.

The next morning the wise men began their journey home. They did not return to the palace of King Herod.

When the wise men had gone, Mary thought again about what the angel had said to her. She picked Jesus up and held him close. She knew that Jesus was very special, and that his birth would always be remembered as a time of great joy and happiness.

All these things appear in the pages of the story.
Can you find them?

angel

inn-keeper

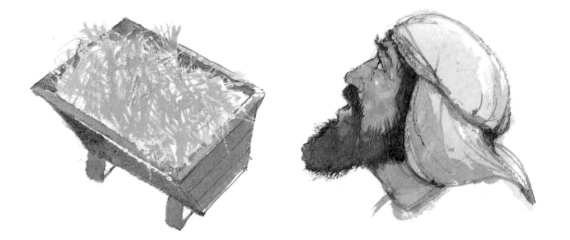

manger

Joseph

sheep

star

wise men

baby Jesus

STORIES FROM THE
LIFE OF JESUS

Jesus grew up in Nazareth, where he lived with his parents. When he was twelve years old he went with them to Jerusalem for the feast of the Passover. There he spent time in the temple with the teachers, talking and listening. The teachers were surprised at how much Jesus already knew.

Jesus had a cousin called John. When John grew up, he left home to live in the wilderness near the river Jordan. There he preached the word of God and soon people flocked to listen to him and to be baptized in the river.

One day Jesus went to the river Jordan to be baptized by John.
"Will you baptize me?" asked Jesus.
"It should be you who baptizes me," replied John, who knew that Jesus was the Son of God.

John baptized Jesus in the river
Jordan and as he finished, a strange
thing happened. The heavens opened
and the spirit of God came down in
the form of a dove. Then the people
watching heard the voice of God say,
"This is my Son, and I am pleased
with him."

After being baptized, Jesus knew that he had God's work to do. He went to live in Galilee, where he began to tell the people about God. One day, as he walked beside the lake, Jesus met two fishermen; Simon called Peter, and Andrew. He would need help in his work so he said to the two men, "Why don't you come with me? Together we can tell the people about God."

So Peter and Andrew joined Jesus. Jesus met two more fishermen called John and James. They also joined him. Soon Jesus had chosen twelve men to help him with God's work. These men were called his disciples or the twelve apostles. They were Peter (Simon), Andrew, John, James, Philip, Thomas, Bartholomew, Matthew, James, Thaddeus, Simon and Judas Iscariot.

Jesus travelled throughout Galilee talking to the people and teaching all the time. Wherever he went, great crowds followed him. His fame spread throughout the country.

As Jesus travelled from town to town, huge crowds would gather to listen to his stories. These stories are called parables, and they helped the people understand how God wanted them to lead their lives.

One story Jesus told was about a rich
man who had two sons. The elder
son was always busy and hard-
working, but the younger son was
very lazy.

One day the younger son said to his father, "Please will you give me my share of the money you intend to leave me when you die." The man did this and the younger son left home.

Instead of spending his money wisely,
he wasted all he had. He bought
himself expensive clothes and gifts,
but never bothered to look for work.
Soon all his money had gone.

Then a terrible famine spread throughout the country. The son was very hungry because he had no money for food. He went to many places looking for work. A farmer gave him the job of looking after his pigs. He was so hungry that he even wanted to eat the food that was given to the pigs.

Then one day the son decided to
return home to his father. "I will tell
him I am sorry, even though I no
longer deserve to be called his son,"
he said.

So the son returned home. When his father saw him he was filled with joy. He ran to his son and hugged him. "Father, please forgive me," said the young man. "I have sinned against you and against God."
But the man was so pleased to have his son back again, he ordered a feast to be prepared.

When the elder son saw that his brother had returned, he was angry. "Why are you preparing a feast?" he asked his father. "My brother wasted all his money." The man saw how upset his son was. "I thought I had lost my son forever," he replied. "But now he is found again." Jesus wanted to show the people that God loves everyone, and forgives those who can say they are sorry.

Another story was about the Good Samaritan.

One day, a man travelling from Jerusalem to Jericho was attacked by robbers. His money and donkey were stolen. He was beaten and left for dead.

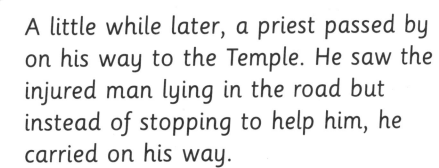

A little while later, a priest passed by on his way to the Temple. He saw the injured man lying in the road but instead of stopping to help him, he carried on his way.

Soon another man passed by. He was a Levite — someone who helped at services in the Temple. He too saw the injured man lying in the road, but carried on his way without even stopping.

A little while after, a man from
Samaria came along the road. When
he saw the injured man he felt sorry
for him and washed his cuts with oil
and wine. Then he helped the man
onto his own donkey and took him to
an inn at the nearest village.

"Here is some money," he told the inn-keeper. "Look after this man. I will come back this way and give you more money if you need it."
Then Jesus asked the crowd, "Which of these men was the true friend?"
"The Samaritan," said the people.
"Then you should be the same," said Jesus. "Always help those who cannot help themselves."

Another story Jesus told was about a
servant who owed his master a great
deal of money.
"Your wife, children and all the land
you own must be sold to pay me,"
said the master.

The servant was terrified.
"Please give me some time," he
begged. "I will pay back all that I
owe you."
The master felt sorry for the man and
forgave him the debt.

A short while later, the same man met a fellow servant who owed him a small amount of money.

"You must pay me what you owe," he said.

"Please give me some time," said the second servant. But the first servant had the man thrown into prison.

The servant's friends were very upset and went to the master to tell him what had happened.
The master was furious and called the servant to him.
"You have been cruel and unkind. I forgave you a debt, can you not forgive a debt, too?"

The servant was thrown into prison. Jesus told his listeners that they too had to learn to forgive one another.

One day Jesus was on a mountain speaking to a huge crowd of people. Jesus taught them many things explaining how they should live according to the rules of God. Jesus told the people to love one another, both friend and enemy.

Jesus also taught the people how to pray, telling them to pray in simple words. Jesus said, "Pray then in this way,

> Our Father who art in Heaven,
> Hallowed be Thy name.
> Thy Kingdom come,
> Thy will be done,
> On earth as it is in Heaven.
> Give us this day our daily bread,
> And forgive us our debts,
> As we forgive our debtors.
> And lead us not into temptation
> But deliver us from evil."

This first prayer that Jesus taught has become known as the Lord's Prayer.

Jesus did many things that an ordinary person could not do. We call these 'miracles'. One of the first miracles happened at a wedding feast in the village of Cana. Jesus' mother, Mary, was also there and while all the guests were enjoying the feast, the wine ran out.

"All the wine has gone," Mary told Jesus. "Can you help? The feast will be spoiled and the bridegroom and his family are very worried."

Jesus noticed a row of empty water jars. "Fill these jars with water," he told the servants, "then pour some out for each of the guests."

The servants did as they were told. As they poured they noticed wine filling all of the cups, and not water.
"Most people serve the best wine first," said one guest to the bridegroom. "You have saved the best until last."

One day a large crowd gathered to listen to Jesus preaching inside a house. Four men arrived, carrying their friend who was unable to move or walk. They tried to reach Jesus but could not find a way through the crowd. Suddenly, one of the four knew how they could reach Jesus. He climbed some steps leading to the roof and made a hole in the roof big enough for his sick friend to pass through.

Then all four friends carried the man onto the roof and with some ropes, lowered him through the hole to the feet of Jesus.

Jesus was pleased with the four friends. They had shown how they believed in him. Then everyone watched in amazement as Jesus healed the man. "Stand up from your mat and walk," said Jesus.
The man stood up and with great joy, walked away.

After this miracle, people flocked to see Jesus, bringing their family and their sick friends with them. Jesus healed many people, even lepers, who were feared by everyone. One day a leper came to Jesus. People would have nothing to do with lepers as they were afraid of catching the disease, leprosy. Jesus knew that lepers were not even allowed into the temple to pray, and he knew that this man was suffering. The man said, "I know that you can heal me," and Jesus saw that the man had faith in him, and he healed him.

Another day, a Roman soldier approached Jesus. He told him he had a servant at home who was very sick. "He is a good and kind man. I do not want him to die," said the soldier.

Jesus asked to be taken to the sick man, but the soldier said that he believed Jesus only had to say the word and the man would not die. Jesus was surprised that the soldier had such great faith, and told him to go home and he would find that the servant was well again.

Once, after preaching to the people all day, Jesus and his disciples were very tired. They decided it was time to rest, so they crossed the lake in their boat. All the people watched them go and began to walk around the shore to meet Jesus. By the time the boat had reached land, there were thousands of people waiting to see Jesus.

Jesus knew how much the people needed him and sat down to talk to them again.

In the evening the disciples said to Jesus, "It is time to rest. The people should leave, but there is nowhere for them to stay and nothing for them to eat."

"Then we must feed them," said Jesus.

"We cannot do that," said one disciple. "There must be five thousand people here."

"Ask if anyone has any food," said Jesus. "Then bring him to me."

After a short time, a little boy was brought to Jesus. "I have five loaves and two fishes," he said. "You may have them." Jesus smiled and said, "Thank you."
The disciples then split the crowd up into groups of fifty. After this, Jesus held up the food for all to see and praised God for it.

Then Jesus handed out some bread and fish to each disciple. No one understood how but as each person was given food, there was always more for the next. Everyone was given food to eat, and all from five small loaves and two fishes.

After Jesus had fed the five thousand,
he persuaded them all to go home.
Then he went into the hills to pray.
The disciples were already rowing
back to the other side of the lake.
Jesus watched the boat
from the top of the hill
and saw that it was
struggling against the
wind. He went down the
hill to help his followers.

Jesus began to walk across the water to the boat. When the disciples saw him, they thought he was a ghost. "It is I!" cried Jesus. "Do not be afraid."

"If it is really you," said Peter, "let me walk out to you."

So Peter began to walk across the water, too. But the wind was very strong, and Peter began to sink. "Lord, save me!" he cried.

Jesus reached out his hand and saved Peter. "Why did you doubt me? Have you no faith?" he asked.

When they climbed into the boat, the wind stopped.

Many people began to believe that Jesus was the Messiah, the Son of God. Jesus talked and listened to the people. He answered their questions by telling them stories to help them understand. Mothers brought their children to Jesus so that he could bless them.

The disciples thought that Jesus had more important people to talk to than the children, but Jesus told them that no one was more important than the children. He told his disciples to let the little children come to him, and he talked to them, held them and blessed them.

To Jesus, the little ones were special.

Soon it was time for the Passover feast, the special festival celebrated by all Jews. Jesus wanted to go to Jerusalem for this special feast. He said to two disciples, "Bring me a donkey that I can ride upon."
So Jesus rode into the great city of Jerusalem on the back of a little donkey.

The people cheered and cried out,
"Hosanna! The Son of God is here!"
They threw branches and leaves at
Jesus' feet, which they had taken
from palm trees. Everyone was happy
that Jesus had arrived.

The following day Jesus went to the temple to pray. There he saw merchants selling their goods and animals. There were also money changers, who were cheating money from the poor. Jesus was very angry.

He overturned all the tables and chased the traders and their animals out of the temple.

"It is written," said Jesus, "my house shall be called a house of prayer. You have made it into a den of thieves!"

The chief priests and teachers did not like Jesus. They thought the people should listen only to them and that Jesus had too many followers. They had been plotting for a long time, trying to think of a way to get rid of him. Caiaphas, the high priest of the temple in Jerusalem, thought they should capture Jesus and hand him over to the Romans.

While they were holding a meeting discussing how to get rid of Jesus, Judas Iscariot came to them. He asked, "How much money will you pay me if I betray Jesus to you?" They paid him thirty pieces of silver to betray Jesus.

To celebrate the Passover, Jesus wanted to eat his last supper with his disciples. He knew that he would be betrayed and put to death. He told them that one of them would betray him but they did not believe him. Jesus washed the feet of his disciples telling them, "Love and care for one another as I have loved you."

Then Jesus gave the blessing. He praised God as he broke the unleavened bread. He gave it to his disciples and said, "This is my body, which I give to you." He poured the wine and said, "This is my blood, which is poured out for many." Jesus was to give his life for the people, so that their sins would be forgiven.

203

After supper, they all left the house and walked towards the Mount of Olives. There Jesus went into the garden of Gethsemane to pray, taking Peter, James and John with him. He asked them to keep watch while he prayed.

Jesus was very troubled and he said to God, "My Father, if it be possible, let this cup pass from me." Jesus was afraid to die but he knew that God's will must be done.

Jesus returned to his disciples but found them asleep. He woke them and said to Peter, "So, could you not watch with me one hour?" He told them to pray and again keep watch. Then Jesus went deeper into the garden and prayed again. Jesus said, "My Father, if there is no other way, Thy will be done." He returned to the disciples and woke them again. He had heard the sound of many people coming and knew that he was going to be betrayed.

A great crowd came into the garden armed with swords and clubs. Judas went up to Jesus and said, "Hail, Master!" and kissed him. Judas had told the priests that the one he kissed would be Jesus, the man they wanted to arrest.

They arrested Jesus and bound his hands. His disciples had run away and Jesus was alone with his enemies. They led him away to Caiaphas, the high priest.

Caiaphas looked at Jesus and asked him if he was the Son of God. Jesus replied, "You say that I am."

The priests said, "He has claimed to be the Son of God. He deserves to die." They could not put Jesus to death since Judea was at that time ruled by the Romans. So they took Jesus to the Roman governor, Pontius Pilate, and told him what Jesus had said.

Pilate listened. Then he asked Jesus if he was the King of the Jews. Jesus replied, "You have said so."
Pilate heard that Jesus was from Galilee which was the province of King Herod. He told the priests to let Herod judge Jesus. So Jesus was taken to Herod, but Herod did not want to judge him either. Jesus was taken back to Pilate.

He was brought before Pilate again
and questioned, but Pilate could not
see any reason why Jesus should be
put to death. The crowd outside were
shouting, "Crucify him! Crucify him!"

Pilate called for a basin of water and washed his hands before the crowd. He said, "I want nothing to do with this, you are responsible." He handed Jesus over to be put to death.

The Roman soldiers took Jesus away.
They beat him and placed a crown of
thorns on his head. They mocked him
and spat on him saying, "Hail, King
of the Jews!"

Jesus was taken out of the city to a place called Golgotha. Jesus was made to carry the cross on which he would be crucified. Jesus was so weak after being beaten, that he fell several times as he carried the heavy cross. A man called Simon of Cyrene was ordered by the soldiers to help Jesus.

The soldiers nailed Jesus to the cross by his hands and feet. Jesus prayed, "Father forgive them, for they know not what they do."

They placed a sign on the cross which read 'Jesus of Nazareth, King of the Jews'. Two robbers were crucified with him.

The soldiers cast lots for the clothing of Jesus. The leaders mocked him saying, "He saved others; let him save himself if he is the Messiah. Come down from the cross so that we may see and believe."

The soldiers also mocked him, offering him sour wine and saying, "If you are the King of the Jews, save yourself."

John, a disciple, stood close by comforting Mary, the mother of Jesus. It had been morning when Jesus was crucified. When it was noon, darkness came over the whole land. At about three in the afternoon Jesus cried out, "My God, my God, why hast thou forsaken me?"

Jesus cried out a second time, "Father, into thy hands I commit my spirit." And then he said, "It is finished." After this, Jesus died.

At the moment Jesus died the earth began to shake and the temple was torn in two from top to bottom. The soldiers were terrified and one of them said, "Truly this man was God's Son."

When evening came, a man called
Joseph of Arimathea went to ask
Pilate if he could take away the body
of Jesus. Pilate was surprised that
Jesus had died so soon and he asked
his soldiers if it was true.
He was told that while
Jesus was on the cross
one of the soldiers had
pierced his side with a
spear, but Jesus was
already dead. Pilate
ordered the body of
Jesus to be given to
Joseph.

Joseph took the body of Jesus from the cross and wrapped Jesus in a linen cloth. Women who had followed Jesus from Galilee and seen him crucified, embalmed his body with the spices.

Then the body of Jesus was placed in a tomb which was cut from the rock in a hillside. They rolled a large rock across the entrance to the tomb. The next day was the Sabbath, when everyone rested according to God's commandment.

The following day, Mary Magdalene and Mary mother of James went to the tomb. Suddenly there was a great earthquake and an angel rolled back the stone from the entrance of the tomb. The angel said, "Do not be afraid, for I know that you seek Jesus who was crucified. He is not here for he has risen." The tomb was empty. The angel told Mary Magdalene to tell the disciples to go to Galilee and that they would see Jesus there.

The disciples went to Galilee where they saw Jesus. He told them that he would always be with them and that they should go and teach the people all that he had taught them. Jesus told them to go and spread the word of God to all nations.

Jesus led the disciples as far as Bethany and lifting his hands, he blessed them. Then Jesus was carried up into heaven.

The disciples did as Jesus asked them to do. They spread the word of God throughout the world.